SPECTRUM®
READERS

LEVEL **3**

ULTIMATE!
Races

By Teresa D

Carson-Dellosa
Publishing

SPECTRUM®

An imprint of Carson-Dellosa Publishing, LLC
P.O. Box 35665
Greensboro, NC 27425-5665

carsondellosa.com

Printed in the USA. All rights reserved.
ISBN 978-1-62399-155-5

01-002131120

Races are competitions of speed, strength, and skill.
Snowboard racers zoom down mountains.
Bicycle racers pedal into the wind.
Motocross racers fly through the mud.
They all want to be the first to finish.

Marathon

A marathon is a race that people run on foot.

The race is 26.2 miles long!

Runners must pace themselves.

They don't want to run out of energy before the race is over.

Runners train for months and months to get ready for a marathon.

Weird Facts

- The Boston Marathon in Massachusetts is a famous race in the United States.

- Paul Tergat ran the fastest marathon in 2003. He ran it in two hours, four minutes, and fifty-five seconds!

Wheelchair Racing

Some athletes race in wheelchairs.
They compete in marathons and
other races.
Wheelchair racers have powerful arms.
Their strong hands turn the
wheels quickly.
Wheelchair racers work hard to train.
They race in wheelchairs that are specially
built to be light and fast.

Weird Facts

- The marathon is an event in the Summer Paralympics. The Paralympics are elite sporting events for athletes with disabilities.

- The Boston Marathon has a wheelchair division.

Swimming

Races can also take place in water.
Swimmers race in large pools.
They also race in lakes, rivers, and oceans.
Some races are short contests of speed.
Other races can be over ten miles long!
Swimmers have lean bodies
and strong muscles.
Their powerful arms and legs move
them through the water.

Weird Facts

- There are four different strokes in swimming races: the backstroke, the breaststroke, the butterfly, and the freestyle.

- Most swimmers swim the front crawl for their freestyle stroke.

Bicycle Race

The most famous bicycle race in the world is called the *Tour de France*.
It lasts for 23 days.
Each day, there is a new race.
The bicycle racer with the fastest times of all the races wins.
Racers ride over 2,000 miles through France and its surrounding countries.

Weird Facts

- The best climber in each Tour de France wears a red polka dot jersey.
- The Tour de France is similar to running a marathon almost every day for three weeks!

Triathlon

The triathlon is one of the toughest races
in the world.
The race is made up of three parts.
Racers swim 2.4 miles.
They bike 112 miles.
Then, they run a full marathon,
which is 26.2 miles!
Triathlon racers must be good
at all three sports.
They swim, bike, and run for miles each week
to get ready for the event.

Weird Facts

- In most triathlons, the three events are back-to-back. A racer's time includes the time it takes to change clothes and shoes.

- The Ironman® World Championship is a famous triathlon in Hawaii.

Snowboard Racing

Snowboard racers surf down
snow-covered mountains.
Sometimes, the racing slope is steep and icy.
Each racer rushes down the slope alone.
The racer makes wide, fast turns.
Poles called *gates* mark where
the racer should turn.
If a racer misses just one gate,
he or she is out of the race.
The racer with the fastest time wins.

- Snowboarding became an Olympic sport in 1998.
- At the 2004 Winter Olympics, American snowboarders won seven medals.

Motocross

Motocross is a motorcycle race
on a dirt track.
The racers ride motorcycles that are
very light but very tough.
They race through ruts and thick mud.
Motocross racers must use skill and
careful planning.
They plan how to pass other racers.
One small mistake, and they could wreck
and lose the race.

Weird Facts

- Motocross is sometimes called *MX* or *MotoX*.
- Motocross racers wear lots of safety
  equipment, including a helmet, goggles,
  boots, and plastic guards for their shins,
  knees, and elbows.

Stock Car Racing

Stock car racing is a sport of speed
and danger.
Drivers must have great skill.
They drive cars around a racetrack
at over 160 miles per hour.
They speed only inches from the other cars.
If a driver loses control, it could mean
a deadly crash.

Weird Facts

- *NASCAR* stands for the "National Association
  for Stock Car Auto Racing." It began in 1948.

- Stock cars used for racing are specially
  made. Each one costs millions of dollars
  to build!

Indy Car Racing

Indy cars are different from stock cars.
Indy cars have "wings" at the front
and back.
They help the car move faster.
The driver's seat is also open to the air.
Indy cars race around a racetrack at
speeds of 200 miles per hour or more.
They get their name from a famous race,
the Indianapolis 500.
This race is 500 miles long!

Weird Facts

- It is tradition for the winner of the Indianapolis 500 to drink milk in the winner's circle.
- Indy car racers go to the track a month ahead of time to do practice laps.

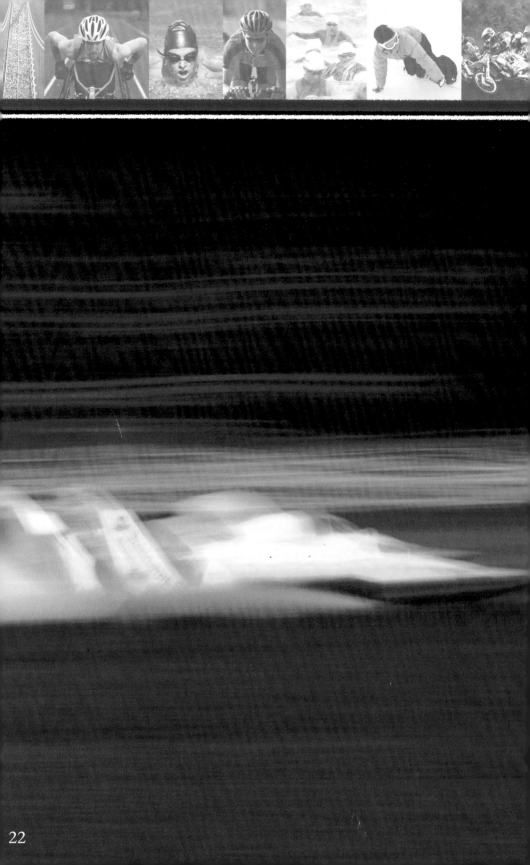

Motorboat Racing

Motorboat racers must be skilled drivers.
Their boats must be in top shape.
Motorboats, called *hydroplanes*, reach speeds
of 200 miles per hour or more.
The racers risk being thrown from the boats.
In some races, the drivers do as many
laps as they can in a set time.
In other races, the drivers go as fast as they
can in a short time.

Weird Facts

- When hydroplane racing first began, it was not uncommon for racers to get hurt or even die. Today, the sport is much safer.

- Some powerful racing boats have four engines.

Yacht Racing

Yachts are fast and graceful on the water.
But racing them in rough seas
can be dangerous.
It takes a skilled team of sailors
to race a yacht.
Sailors can fall overboard, or the yacht
could overturn.
One of the world's most famous yacht
races is called the *America's Cup*.

Weird Facts

- The best boat builders and sailors in the world take part in the America's Cup.

- In 1983, an Australian yacht won the America's Cup. The United States had won the cup for 126 years straight before that.

Hot Air Balloon Racing

Hot air balloons may look peaceful
as they float in the sky.
But racing a hot air balloon is not easy.
The pilot must watch the weather carefully.
He or she must pay attention to the wind.
The balloon is very hard to steer.
Strong winds and storms can pull a balloon
off the racecourse and cause a crash.

Weird Facts

- There are over 7,000 hot air balloons in the United States.

- In some races, hot air balloon teams must steer very close to targets on the ground and then drop weights on them.

Horse Racing

Racehorses are very powerful, fast animals.
They weigh over 1,000 pounds.
Their hooves sound like thunder
as they run around a racetrack.
Racehorse riders are called *jockeys*.
They know their horses well.
A jockey must be able to control his or her
horse during the race.
A fall from a racehorse could be deadly.

Weird Facts

- The Triple Crown is the most famous prize for horse races in America.

- The Triple Crown is made up of three races: the Kentucky Derby, the Preakness, and the Belmont Stakes.

Sled Dog Racing

In sled dog racing, people and animals race together.

The driver of the sled is called a *musher*. The musher's team of dogs pulls the sled throughout the race.

The Iditarod is the world's most famous sled dog race.

It takes place in Alaska each year. Mushers and their teams of dogs race on icy, snowy trails for days and days.

- The Iditarod is over 1,000 miles long. It takes more than a week, sometimes two weeks, to complete it.

- If a musher gets hurt or stuck during an Iditarod, other mushers always stop to help.

ULTIMATE! Races
Comprehension Questions

1. What is a race?

2. How long is a marathon?

3. Why do you think wheelchair racers have powerful arms?

4. Name four places swimmers can race.

5. What is the name of the most famous bicycle race in the world? How long does it last?

6. What three events make up a triathlon?

7. Where do snowboard racers compete?

8. Which is faster: Stock car racing or Indy car racing?

9. How many miles long is the Indianapolis 500?

10. How can yacht racing be dangerous?

11. Who are jockeys?